RECLAMATION

Poems & Reflections

Nancy Viera

Copyright © 2024 Nancy Viera

All rights reserved. De Colores Publishing

Denver, Colorado

Cover art by Cindy Loya, "Te Adoro" 2022

ISBN: 979-8-3306-8134-1

All work depicted is fictional. Names and locations have been altered.

For my son James, I love you
You are enough, you are loved

Also by Nancy Viera
The Grief and The Happiness
Silhouette
Chicago and You
Serendipity

The Moon and I	17
Diary Entry: 3	19
Diary Entry: 4	21
Christmas Gift	23
Hope	25
Reclamation	27
Mother	29
Tamales and Melancholy	31
Relics	33
Evidence	35
Done with you	37
Cave	39
Diary Entry 1	41
Diary Entry 2	43
Rant	45
The Medicine	47
A Heart of Jazz	49
Lifetimes	51
Summer Heat	53
La Magia de tu Mirada	55
Media Luna	57
Parker Road	59
Snow Day	61
Crispy Potatoes	63

From Alma to Jacob 65
From Monica 67
My Universe 69
Empty Shelf 71
House of Spirits 73
You Are History 75
Eternity 77
Of Dolores and Borders: A Short Story
                                 79
Thank you 89

RECLAMATION

Poems & Reflections

Nancy Viera

With Abandonment comes Reclamation!

Reclamation is more than a poetry collection to me; it is a reflection of my own journey through abandonment and the process of finding my way back to myself. Writing these poems allowed me to explore the emotional and spiritual weight of loss and absence, but also the strength and beauty that come from reclaiming our power. I wanted this collection to be a companion for anyone who has ever felt abandoned, reminding them that while others may leave, they do not have to leave themselves behind. Abandonment comes in many forms: the absence of someone we love, the end of a relationship, a loss of connection with society or even ourselves. At its core, abandonment shakes our sense of security and belonging. I know what it feels like to sit in the silence, to be overwhelmed by the weight of what's missing. But what I have learned—and what I hope my readers will see—is that the silence is where we hear ourselves most clearly.
In writing *Reclamation*, I wanted to give words to the pain that so often goes unspoken. It's an experience many carry but don't always feel comfortable sharing. By naming it, by putting it on the page, I hoped to validate not only my own feelings but those of anyone who might feel lost in the aftermath of someone walking away.
This collection is, at its heart, an invitation to self-reflect. Writing these poems taught me not to shy away from the pain of abandonment but to face it fully and let it guide me back to my strength. For so long, I

believed that my healing depended on someone else returning, on receiving the answers or closure I thought I needed. But I learned that healing begins within, when we realize that no one has the power to take away our worth.

One of the greatest lessons abandonment taught me was how to be okay with people leaving my life. It wasn't an act of defeat but a moment of liberation. When I wrote, *"Let all the pain become ashes / Reclaim / Let new flowers grow instead,"* it was a declaration of growth. I realized that even in the wake of loss, there is fertile ground to start anew.

Abandonment has a way of making us feel fragmented, like pieces of ourselves were taken along with the person who left. Through these poems, I worked to reclaim those parts of myself. Writing became a way to put the pieces back together, not as they were before, but in a way that was truer, stronger, and more whole.

Reclaiming myself meant refusing to let others define my story. It meant seeing myself not as broken but as resilient. The lines in this collection are a testament to that resilience—to the strength it takes to begin again and to rediscover the power that already lives inside us.

When we're abandoned, closure isn't always given to us; sometimes we have to create it for ourselves. Writing *Reclamation* allowed me to find that closure, to forgive where I needed to forgive, and to release the weight of what no longer served me. I came to understand that closure is not about forgetting; it's about freeing ourselves.

I hope these poems remind readers that while abandonment leaves wounds, those wounds can heal. Even after loss, life continues. As I wrote, *"The earth swallows all your fears / Leaves you with new roots,"* I realized that we are capable of rebuilding, of allowing new life to grow where the old was taken. *Reclamation* is not just my story—it's for anyone who has felt left behind, unseen, or unheard. Writing this collection was my way of finding peace and reclaiming my voice. I hope it inspires others to do the same: to embrace their solitude, heal their wounds, and step into their power with courage and grace. There is also a few love poems, because would it really be if I didn't include some love poems? Abandonment is not the end of our story. It is where we begin again. These poems are proof that even in the darkest moments, we can reclaim ourselves and find beauty in our resilience. We are enough. We deserve love.

THE MOON AND I

The essence of this life
Lives in between my curls
It calls me divine
Beautiful and eternal
Every inch of my thick skin
Dances with the sonorous light
I rise above the Rocky Mountains
Like my life depends on it
Like the moon is my friend
She says here child follow me
Pour your light above the peaks
Lift your voice above
You'll never be struck again
By the lighting of their rejection
You live here now
Hear your reclamation

Nancy Viera

DIARY ENTRY: 3

Allowing the flow in is such a new and beautiful feeling.
Being surprised by good things,
and good feelings to show up is surprising me.
It all fits in.
It's what I deserve.
And maybe before I didn't allow it
or love myself at the level I am now.
But, I am here now.
I love myself.
I welcome in the flow, the good.
The peace, the unlimited abundance
 that has always been available to me.
It is joy, and love,
and I am so grateful for this new chapter in my life.

Nancy Viera

DIARY ENTRY: 4

Finding out that allowing the flow of life happens also means being okay with people to walk out of your life like water, quick and clear, was not expected so soon. It's not the first time. She's done it many times.

This time it is final.

When my mother sprung up to follow one of the few people who have hurt me the most, my sister. Without any question, no goodbye, nothing. That was the explanation. Silence is enough to cut my heart.

No matter what, I am very proud of myself. It felt so good to stand up for myself and keep my sacred space. I no longer have to have anxiety over them. I can, and I do, feel safe and free now.

I was never enough for them to love me in their eyes.

But, in mine, the most important, I am enough. I am loved.

CHRISTMAS GIFT

When I was 3 she left
Abandoned without regret
Then when she came back she promised happy days
It started with a rancid lipstick for my fifteenth birthday
Then a slap on the face because lipstick is for whores
You're a whore
When I moved out
Oh surprise
Slap
What do you mean?
I hope the next time I see you is in a casket
I hope you die
Slap
It's your fault your husband slept with your sister
Your poor sister
She says
She coddles the sister
Slap
Then he died
The husband
and she took me in
The little girl felt safe again
A perfume for a gift
A rancid perfume
Here take these diet pills

Nancy Viera

You are not enough
Slap
Then, one year it was toilet paper
You should be happy, it's from Costco!
You owe me everything
I immigrated
I assimilated
You owe me your light
Slap
Then I said, that's enough!
I am enough
And I never looked back.

HOPE

She hit me a million times
A million times
I forgave her
She dragged me one more time
And one more time
I forgave her
Because the elixir of her food
The aromas of a
False home
False hope
Because I kept waiting
Hopeful
That one day
When she stops hitting me
She will say
I love you

Nancy Viera

RECLAMATION

You sit with your head up to the sky
Wild curls snake all around
While you shed the skin of the old you
The time is now
And you say,
"What an honor to become who I am meant to be.
The earth swallows all your fears
Leaves you with new roots
All is new
So you take the leap
And after all these years
17 years
Instead of picking them,
You pick yourself first.

Nancy Viera

MOTHER

I am the parent that stayed
The one who fought all the demons
Slayed them every morning
when they tried to weaken my spirit
I didn't coward to the pain
I didn't fail my strength
I remained
And I love
And I am tender
And still I fight
I will not fail as a parent
Because he deserves the world
I will stay

Nancy Viera

Reclamation

TAMALES AND MELANCHOLY

The corn husk melt
Like silk through my skin
I am made of tamales
And tamales I make
Every 12th of December
before the Christmas lights twinkle
The copal burns and
All around the faithful you'll hear
La Guadalupana
La Guadalupana
Bajo al Tepeyac
We sing to the Virgen of Guadalupe
Then we let the chile soak, the dreams cook
And the memories rise with the steam of the pots and
Every year I miss you more
I miss your story telling
You're big Stetson hat
I even miss the smell of tequila on your breath
I am pulled in by the traditions
And pulled away by the strings
My grandmother tied around my heart
Shades of red and of green wrap my heart
The heart that remembers what the land cried for
How many battles it lost
How many battles I won

Nancy Viera

To be here today
Softening the lines between tradition
And new stories
Feliz Navidad Feliz Navidad

RELICS

In the quiet of the snow storm
I found pieces left behind
by my ancestors
A voice
A set of strong legs
Music made of gold
And a heart to carry it all
The whisper of love
Lingers above my head
Guiding me through
The foggy nights
charged with magic
I am the first to move and love
Different than all of them
New and shiny
Not a chingona
But a cabrona yes
Because that's more powerful
That's one that breaks the
molds and the silence
A cabrona rises above the dust
And never settles
She seems unbreakable
The truth is I don't want to be
A cabrona or a chingona

I want to be soft
Like a flower under the moon
And still
Heal
So I do it
I heal and I mend
And I honor their love

EVIDENCE

When I walk back into town
I will not care about
The dimples on every inch of my body
Carved by their voices
These carvings
They used to carry the
"What will they say"
Every step I took, I cared
I collected their words
until I couldn't anymore so
I poured out the words
Left them by the river
The river that witnessed so many crossings
It watched as I left the town again and again
It cut me with the sharp curve
 every time
I walked back to town
This time
When I walk by every house
I'll thank them for teaching me
What not to be
I break any spells
That bound me to the land
I am who I am meant to be
Not

Nancy Viera

What they want me to be

Reclamation

DONE WITH YOU

I wonder what your face would look like now
8 years later.
Would you have gray hair too?
Or any hair at all.
How did time affect you?
If you were still alive
I still miss you
Almost everyday, I think
I wonder what you would be doing
8 years later
If you were still alive
How many times would the winds blow you my way
How many times you'd walk away again
If you were still alive
I'd like to say I've healed but,
The scar stares and stabs at me every
time I see you in your sons eyes
The uncanny resemblance startles me sometimes
And I wonder if it's you visiting us
Checking in on us
Have we changed
Do we still miss you
Are you a ghost lingering
I made it to Spain

Nancy Viera

Without you
I smiled and cried
Without you
I wonder if you would be happy with who I am now
If you were still alive

CAVE

I would be remiss
If we continue to exist
And I continue to wander ...
Do you think that maybe
I could be the one that fills the cave behind your heart?
When will we allow these paths to finally cross?
Moon rays light the path
Can you take it?
Can I?

Nancy Viera

DIARY ENTRY 1

When defining happiness,
I find myself in the constant pull between
myself and my so called purpose.
There has been a strange pull.
It doesn't feel bad, but it also doesn't feel good.
It's very neutral.
I suppose.
 It's very neutral…why?
I am not sure what I need to work on
I feel like I am looking for my inherent guidance.
When I regulate my thoughts I find myself.
I look for guidance in my dreams,
even in the outlandish.
How many more affirmations do I need to say?
How to define anything.
I think that's okay.

DIARY ENTRY 2

It is important to remind ourselves that while others abandon us
In their ways of survival
We must not abandon ourselves
Whatever peoples role in our lives,
they have boundaries and it will not always align with yours.
Comeback to yourself and be confident
that the only person who will always be there for you
to survive is you.
You can always count on yourself
And that is how you survive abandonment.
That is how you walk through life.
With you.
You are enough.

RANT

There is a constant unfairness of how fairness is distributed among humans. The idea of equality is fake and it only provides a sense of hope that one day fairness will be distributed evenly.

Is false hope all we have to hold on to? The idea that eventually we will all be treated, get away with, and have the privilege *some* people do?

Not only is it false hope, it is fuel. The fuel I use everyday, to stand up. Even in the face of uncertainty.

There is no way I will be silent. I do not know how to remain silent. Read me my rights.

Arrest me all you want.

What's the point of having a voice. If it's uncomfortably received, I can't control that.

No one else holds the key to my destiny or can pave the way for me. I am the only one that can do that. I can decide which way to go. So when unfairness is present, I will make the uncomfortable present too.

You might sit in your privilege, but it will be uncomfortable when I am around. Even when you think you have the key to my success.

Not today. Not tomorrow.

I belong to myself.

Nancy Viera

THE MEDICINE

Let all the pain become dust
Dust that turns into flowers
Let the moon rays guide you and heal you
And with the waves of the ocean,
Let me love you
Let all the pain become ashes
Reclaim
Let new flowers grow instead
Let their be calm
And don't ever forget that you are,
The medicine

Reclamation

A HEART OF JAZZ

I've returned to the cities you
 once made me hate
Because of the way you talked to me
I've reclaimed them
with every step
Every bite of food
Every stranger I kissed
and danced with
When you made me feel small
I ripped my heart out
This time
I went back and picked it up
I've let the powdered sugar
of New Orleans beignets transport me
From the pained state you left me in
To the vibrant full of life
woman I am
and
jazz in my heart
Is all I have now

LIFETIMES

A quick collection of my thoughts
Takes me through thousands and thousands of lifetimes
And in everyone of them,
I find a piece of my heart
I pick it up
So that when I glue it back with love
It will be easier in this lifetime
Everything flows
Everything has arrived
Now.

Nancy Viera

SUMMER HEAT

Would it be possible
If by the end of this summer
We can sit in the back of your car
And kiss?
I want to feel you on me
Inside me
All around me
I am curious to learn how my curves tense up
When you all your tongue on my skin
I want to get lost in the waterfalls with you
Reaching secret points only you know about
It could take hours, and hours, and hours
And, I will still surrender to you
If I wasn't ready then,
I am now
Come for me

Nancy Viera

LA MAGIA DE TU MIRADA

There is magic in your eyes
They suspend me in the air
Tus ojos de oro
In between kissing
And being enchanted
Your lips strike me like a match
You light it all up
And
Eventually
Eventually will arrive
Eventually is here
I don't want to be a collector of kisses
I want to be your keeper
I want to swim forever
In the magic of your eyes

Nancy Viera

MEDIA LUNA

I admire the half moon
La media luna
More than the full moon?
Oh yes
I admire the ways she is part of two
worlds and the way she waltzes from darkness to light
The way you hang in two places at once
She makes me feel like I could move mountains
I do move mountains
You make me feel like a mountain
And sometimes I feel like a fire lives inside me
It consumes me
Like you do

Nancy Viera

PARKER ROAD

I can hear the traffic
The loud muffler,
I can hear the shopping carts pushed against the others
Then he pulls me in
Tucks a curl behind my ear
I can taste the sauce on his lips
The desire is salty and delicious
I can feel his tongue reaching down for my heart
His hands smooth the line between my neck and my cheek
Claiming me
And when I can feel my breath escaping
I open my eyes
To be knocked away by his golden eyes
He takes me and cradles me, I melt on his chest
I am lost in the sense of his safety

SNOW DAY

I want to sit here
Only here
With you by my side
Reading your book, reading me
Watching the snow pile outside our window
The window we look at every time the full moon calls
I want you to wrap me in a million kisses
Like the million snowflakes wrap the ground
I love hiding from the world
Here
With you
Only you

CRISPY POTATOES

I remember the day a man fell in love with me
We were cooking breakfast potatoes
He was mad they didn't brown
I said "add butter"
They turned crispy
He looked at me
At the crispy potatoes
He told me he loved me
Kissed me
Lost me in his blue eyes
Then
He ghosted me

FROM ALMA TO JACOB

You can't stop him
He is the light undone that blankets over my sky.
When I'm scared, his very beautiful eyes envelop me in love
and I forget what fears troubled me.
I could tell you a million times he's my beacon.
I am never lost.
The moment our souls merged
 I fell for every curve of his heart, his face.
In his body I relish the years and if could freeze our mornings,
drinking coffee, drinking his essence,
I would be in heaven.
I am in his heaven.
Every time I sing he holds me time after time.
Dances my dreams through his soul.
I gave him my heart, he gave me sweet surrender.
He is my everything.
My home.
My valentine.

Nancy Viera

FROM MONICA

I prayed for the day I'd get to be in love with you.
You went away, came back, I left you, but this time you stayed.
Countless nights imagining what it would be like to know
what it's like to see you linger
 in between my dreams and my reality.
When you walk by, I thank the universe for the essence of you.
When I dream, you sneak in just to see if I am safe,
then you join me and we dance.
I love dancing with you,
let them watch, all that matters is I've found you.
Will you be my forever?
My reason to smile
My home?
My valentine?

MY UNIVERSE

When you sit and listen to me
A universe of constellations and planets
And uncertain places
Unleash above my head
Takes off like a train
You follow me
You hear me
You take my hand and go anywhere with me
I know that when you hold me
You hold my voice and my heart
You help me rewrite stories
And then you make yourself fit in right in between
All these moments when I needed you the most
You are here now
When you listen to me
I know you hear me
All of me,
And I am,
All yours

EMPTY SHELF

I have this messy closet
Full of clothes and coats
And shoes and dresses, many dresses
Colorful dresses, silky blouses
Blouses I've never worn
Some are hanging
Some are folded
Some lay on the floor
And when I look at my messy closet, I am scared
Scared that you will not fit in there
With your coats and cardigans
And your boots
I am scared I've folded my heart all wrong
Like the messy closet
And that nothing will fit here
I am scared that your shelf will stay empty
And that maybe you'll never leave
Even when it's messy
Your pressed white shirt will hang
Next to my white dress
And then maybe
I will not be scared
Because you love me
And I love you

Nancy Viera

HOUSE OF SPIRITS

House of Spirits by Isabel Allende lays opens on my bed
Page 106 awaits for my return
106, the number of days I've thought about you
106 days waiting to see if just for a moment,
You come lay next to me
Pick me up
Linger on the page
Read me like a book
Caress every letter of my story
Pick up a pen, write on my margins
Tell me how you would do it
How you would kiss me and never put me down
You and I are timeless,
A classic
When you turn to the last page,
It will not say
The End.

Nancy Viera

YOU ARE HISTORY

I'd write about you
Until my hands fell off
Until the last sunset
In the history of books
The time in between breaths
I find you
Restless and unforgettable
Your love taste like coffee
Like endless mornings together
During the long days
The good days the bad ones
You are my refuge
My safe haven
I've memorized you
Like the maps of all
The cities I've visited
With the illusion that
You'd be there
In the middle of it all
Waiting for me
To write about you
Until my heart falls off

Nancy Viera

ETERNITY

I want to kiss you
Waste my time with you
Keep your secrets
Adore you
Love you
Your essence is my elixir
You strum me like a violin
Gentle and precise
You open me like a book
It is my pleasure to be read by you
To welcome my wrinkles with you
The gray that sparkles our hair together
I knew I'd never forget you
I never will
You are my eternity
My forever

Nancy Viera

OF DOLORES AND BORDERS: A SHORT STORY

    With the help of a few strange men with long mustaches and bright yellow caps, my fourteen-year-old brother Carlos and I were led through the scorching desert of Arizona. The heat like lightning bolts on my back struck hate for my mother. Each sweat dropped down my face enraged me. I counted the steps in between breaths, telling myself my breath is the only thing I can control. How many others had told themselves the same only to meet their demise. My Mother insisted I follow my brothers across the border to pursue a dream of hers, I never even thought about being a nurse.

    When we arrived in California, our uncle waited for us standing tall with a shaved head. "Ahora si, a chingarle!" He said with a smile on his face, time to work hard. Before I could get used to the heat of California, which was much more rancid than the one in my hometown in Chihuahua just miles and borders away. I yearned for the ocean also just miles away fro me. I started working in a kitchen washing dishes and doing most of the cleaning. The smells of the kitchen would dance around my face, provoking my nose into a salacious delight. I watched the cooks effortlessly move from one vegetable to another, slicing each with precise cuts, throwing them into the sizzling pans and sliding them on plates that would steam with deliciousness. This is what my dreams look like, I thought. Not my mother's wishes of being a nurse.

    Back in my uncles' garage, the makeshift apartment he

provided for Carlos and me, the cold oatmeal invited me to start the day. I played with it by adding extra ingredients I would find at the little store a few blocks away full of groceries and gossip. The clerk never smiled at me. Long walks around the block taking in the sounds and smells of the big city brought melancholy to my heart. So different from the little town I grew up in with hills surrounding it. I missed the morning mist but the oatmeal would be my solace.

During a morning shift at the kitchen, one of the cooks noticed me watching him. Santos was a flirty green-eyed man from El Salvador, and I liked him. He'd often catch me watching him cook while I lowered my eyes and kept washing the dishes wondering what it would take to touch his face while running my fingers through his curls.

One sunny and hazy afternoon he invited me out to dinner and I gleefully obliged. Getting used to the haze was another new thing living in Los Angeles. We spent many afternoons walking around Echo Park eating paletas, slurping up their cold malty deliciousness talking and dreaming, sometimes kissing and holding hands.

"What are your dreams, Lolis? Why are you in Los Angeles?" He asked as he licked the cheese off his fingers from the nachos he was scarfing down.

I told him I was here to save money and go to nursing school so I could go back to my small town and help the sick there. The town is secluded in the Sierra Madre hills, making it hard for doctors, ambulances, or any type of help to arrive on time. The elderly often die before any help arrives. I thought maybe this would be how my Mother wanted me to help. My eyes dropped down to the earth, I felt my dreams slip away into the cracks of the cement below my feet.

Santos quickly rejected the idea, he could see the disappointment in my eyes and asked again, tilting my chin up to meet his eyes. This time I was honest with him.

"I want to own a restaurant, I want to cook all day and make people happy with my food. Then when I am a tired viejita, I want to live in a small ranch, with chickens and goats and a big garden with tons of begonias, rose bushes, and vegetables. Or maybe by the beach, or the mountains, I just want to ne happy." I felt like jumping up and down thinking about it. I could feel my heart beating faster in fear, thinking about doing anything against my mama's wishes. I looked down at my worn-down black converse sneakers and woke up from my daydream.

"It will happen," he lifted my chin again and this time kissed me, "you will probably have a few kids, too."

I fell into a dream.

We welcomed our little Marisela not long after the walks and the kissing. We fell in love. Marisela's beautiful dark hair covered her head and she had green eyes like her father's. Santos was immediately in love. We moved into Inez's garage in East Los Angeles. Inez was from the same town as me and she charged us two hundred dollars a month. Santos took good care of Marisela and me. Even in the small garage he made me feel like a queen. The space was small, the love felt big.

Taking up the breeze of the evening I sat on the porch with little Marisela in my arms when Santos showed up in a brand new red chevy truck. I did not question where he got the money to pay for it. I was in pure bliss of being a new mom and he was providing. Blind to any red flags.

He told me he had picked up a few extra shifts at the restaurant and was coming up on top, so why would I question it.

Guilt made its way into my life again. It had been a year since I had decided to call my Mother who was livid with how my life was turning out. "That is not what I sent you up there to do, Dolores. What will people say?"

That is what she cares about? I thought.

"Bring the little one to me, I want to meet her, but don't bring him. I could care less about that man."

Santos loved the idea of me taking a trip to Mexico to see my parents. He suggested that I leave the little one with them for a few months so I could return to the states and we could go on a trip together. Once I returned to my hometown my Mother completely forgot about me and was enamored with Marisela's curls and chubby cheeks that she did not protest when I asked if I could leave the chunky girl to her care. I kissed both of them on the forehead not knowing I wouldn't return to them any time soon.

******

Months later, I woke up from a cold sweat in the middle of the night, I looked around the unfamiliar dark prison cell and for a second forgot why I was there. I panicked and looked for a way out, only to find out the reality of my fate. I was locked up in Costa Rica, my home for the next seven years.

Santos told me to pack lightly for our trip, we were going out of the country but assured me Costa Rica was hot and I would only need a bathing suit and a few summer dresses to have a good time. The humidity slapped me in the face as we stepped off the airplane, my hair poofed up. I kept trying to calm it down to no avail. The frizz won. I welcomed the heat as we settled into our hotel room. Santos told me to take a dip in the pool as he ran errands in town. A few of his friends lived nearby and he wanted to say hi. I didn't protest, a cool pool to myself was just what I needed. By the time Santos returned a floral dress draped down my body. He took it off and we made love into the dawn. The days went by like reading a romance novel. We'd eat fruit in the hammock taking in the sounds of the world around us. The walks by the beach felt like a dream as we dipped our toes in the water, ending up with a swim in the moonlight. We were so in love.

The romantic getaway soon came to an end, and I craved the humidity before leaving it. When we were in line for customs in Costa Rica to return to the United States, an officer approached me and told me I would need to be searched in a different room.

I was scared and asked Santos to come with me, he ignored me and looked down at the floor as he didn't know who I was as if I wasn't his daughter's mother. I pleaded for him to look at me as the officer took me into the room. That was the last time I saw Santos in my life. My heart broke into a million pieces.

The officer found several pounds of illegal substances in my bag. I was handcuffed, confused, and heartbroken. The judge sentenced me to ten years in prison for illegal substance trafficking.

After six months I was able to get a hold of my parents and told them what happened. My mother hung up the phone and would not take my calls for the next five years. I wondered what she was telling all those people whose approval she needed where the mother of her granddaughter was at. I stood next to the phone soaking in shame and guilt.

I quickly got involved in volunteer work at the prison. It was an all-women prison, most of them were in for the same charges as I was. I helped decorate for the Christmas parties and made tamales for all of us to share. I'd help my cellmates take care of their kids when they were brought in for weekend visitation. I pictured my curly-haired Marisela all grown up and romanticized the idea of one day reuniting.

I would make a phone call every month to no avail. My mother wanted nothing to do with me and for a few moments, I forgot I was also a Mother. I let my inhibitions run wild and would entertain the idea of any man or any woman who would glance my way. Where else was I going to find love?

Two years later I was notified that my mom processed all the necessary steps to have me extradited to Mexico. A few months later I arrived in the heat of the Summer in the desert city of Chihuahua.

My mom and Marisela would take a bus that took almost 8 hours to get from the small town in the middle of the sierra to the city. Marisela told me the smell of the cleaner made her sick and she threw up every time. She was sick of having to travel every Friday to see me for one day. My mother took me aside and also expressed her disgust with having to go through a full-body search every weekend and in between looks of disgust threaten me that she would stop visiting. She said it was my turn to make an effort to get out of there. Her threats were my fuel, she was right. I used all the resources available to get an early release from my sentence. I continued to volunteer for work, those bathroom tiles were never cleaner.

Four years went by when I arrived in Namiquipa on a dusty afternoon, nauseous and ready for a shower. I finally understood why Marisela hated the bus ride so much, they used too much purple fabuloso. I was embraced by her sweet smile, my mother's cold scolding eyes, and my father's stern handshake. I immediately realized I needed to find a source of income and crossing the border was going to be expensive. I managed to save a hefty amount of money throughout my imprisonment but not enough to pay for a bus ride and a room when I got there. I was not going back to my uncle in Los Angeles.

I found a way to buy wholesale clothing and sell them for twice the price to the rich ladies in Namiquipa. They would gather in their expensive living rooms trying on outfit after outfit. I'd listen in their gossip in between clinks of coffee mugs about the whereabouts of so and so's daughter. I wondered if they talked about me this way when I was gone. Did they know where I had been just months before? Did they care, like my Mother always scolded me for?

After many fashion parties I finally had enough for me to leave, this time I would take my curly-haired girl with me. We arrived in Colorado a few bus rides later, this time welcomed by my brother Carlos who was now married and had a beautiful little boy. He had also started his own trucking business and owned two roaring trucks that hauled all types of material around Denver. Marisela and I stayed in his spare bedroom for a few months before I put a deposit down on a one-bedroom apartment on the north side of Denver overlooking Sloans Lake. The first piece of furniture I bought was a lamp I got at a yard sale. Zuly, my brother's wife, was keen on second-hand sales and took me shopping with her every Saturday morning until our apartment was fully furnished. The second hand furniture reminded of me of smells from Los Angeles, melancholy would melt in my dreams.

Marisela started school that fall and quickly settled into her English as a Second Language class. I was once again washing dishes, this time staying away from the flirty men.

Long shifts and long nights paid off when I purchased my first roach coach and stocked it with everything I needed to feed the hungry workers building new skyscrapers in Downtown Denver. Marisela would help me fill up cups of salsa the night before, while I made three hundred breakfast burritos. With drinks and other snacks, I was bringing home close to one thousand dollars a day.

It felt like I was breaking my back, day in and day out to make sure Marisela had all she needed and keep her motivated to stay in school. She was doing so good, we had it figured out.

Or so I thought. One gray rainy day she called me from an abortion clinic. She needed me to pick her up. I was furious and confused, when did my baby grow up that all of the sudden she is making life and death decisions? When I got there she was sitting in the waiting room, rolled up in a ball, her eyes puffy and red. "I didn't do it, Mom, I am keeping the baby."

A swollen-belly Marisela soon delivered the most beautiful, gentle, baby girl. My daughter's boyfriend was by her side every step of the way. I could see they were so in love, and I craved that type of love for myself. Instead, I focused on helping with babysitting, cleaning, and cooking meals for them. In the blink of an eye, the little family moved out into a place of their own and I found my apartment empty without them. I longed for the days filled with baby cries, the smells of food cooking and the radio blasting cumbias. I was on my own for the first time.

I began to explore Colorado more. It started with small hikes in Evergreen. I'd get lost at first and it became such an adventure, every trail led to beautiful views and my lungs craved the fire. One late summer misty morning, I laced up my brown hiking boots, grabbed my backpack full of snacks and water, and decided to hike up to Mount Evans. About half-way through the fourteen thousand-mile trek to the summit I stopped in my tracks. What was I thinking going up a mountain by myself? My mother's voice rang loud and clear in my head.

"I didn't send you to the states to enjoy, I sent you to work!"

I shook it off fast and continued my hike up. I felt stronger than ever and I was going to make it no matter what. When I finally arrived at the summit of Mount Evans my legs were what I was most grateful for at the moment. I stood at the top of the mountain, sweating, parched, hungry, and with a full heart. I began to cry, sweat trickled down my back and my neck when I heard some steps closing in my way. I turned around to find a rugged blonde man smiling at me.

"Hi there, good job hiking it up." I thanked him, smiled reluctantly, and began my trek down the mountain after taking many snaps of the panorama in front of me.

For some reason, the man's presence remained with me throughout the sweaty walk down the mountain. It was not uneasy, he felt familiar. When I got back to the parking lot and took a few minutes to gather myself and prepare for the drive back home the man was doing the same in the truck parked next to me. He smiled again, this time I approached with no reluctance.

"I am Lola, what's your name?" I smiled.

Dale was a seasoned hiker and offered me some tips. By the end of our conversation, we exchanged numbers and agreed to meet for beers sometime soon back in Denver.

I met up with Dale at a noisy brewery downtown in the Ri-No district. At least that's what all the new folks were calling it, I knew it by Five Points. More lively people used to live there. Dale told me all about his adventures. He had moved to the states twenty years back leaving his home and parents back in Argentina. We had a lot in common, our native language and our families expecting us to save them, waiting for us in another country. Dale surprised me when he told me what he did for a living.

"I own ten lunch trucks," he said with pride in his eyes. I couldn't believe it and gleefully told him about mine.

"I knew you looked familiar, I have seen your truck around," he said with a smile on his face.

A brief romance and a quick courthouse wedding later, Dale and I were living our dreams together. We bought a house in the bustling Berkley neighborhood. Soon a chicken coop and a small garden were up and running in the backyard. I was happy. I dreamed of this.

As I was tending to my garden one early fall evening, the phone rang. I brushed the dirt and sweat from my forehead, clicked to accept the call, as I caught my breath the familiar voice of a man came through,

"I want to meet my granddaughter, Dolores."

My heart stopped.

THANK YOU

Thank you for picking up Reclamation. Thank you for your support as I wait for my yes, to publish Flower Moon Runner, a novel.

I hope you find a little bit of yourself in these pages. I hope that you too find those ways to reclaim yourself.

You are enough.

Mil gracias.

Nancy Viera is a Mexican American author from Denver, Colorado. She is the author of a memoir, The Grief and The Happiness, and has written three poetry collections, Silhouette, Chicago and You and Serendipity. She is the host of City Silhouettes, a local artist showcase and belongs to the Colorado Poets Center. Nancy writes both in English and Spanish. She has been an Ofrendas Workshop Facilitator with the Latino Cultural Arts Center and her work has been showcased at the Denver Art Museum.

Follow her on Instagram at omgnancita or www.nancymviera.com

Photo by Ashley Reed

Reclamation

www.ingramcontent.com/pod-product-compliance
Lightning Source LLC
LaVergne TN
LVHW031614060526
838201LV00065B/4832